PLAYING
PRO
SPORTS

PLAYING PRO
HOCKEY

Jeff Hawkins

Lerner Publications Company • Minneapolis

Lerner Publications Company
A division of Lerner Publishing Group, Inc.
241 First Avenue North
Minneapolis, MN 55401 USA

For reading levels and more information, look up this title at
www.lernerbooks.com.

Content Consultant: Mark Parrish, 12-year NHL veteran

MAR 2 3 2015

Library of Congress Cataloging-in-Publication Data

Hawkins, Jeff.
    Playing pro hockey / by Jeff Hawkins.
      pages    cm. — (Playing pro sports)
    Includes index.
    ISBN 978–1–4677–3847–7 (lib. bdg. : alk. paper)
    ISBN 978–1–4677–4729–5 (eBook)
    1. Hockey—Juvenile literature.  2. Professional sports—
Juvenile literature.  I. Title.
  GV847.25.H39  2015
  796.962'64—dc23                        2013048332

Manufactured in the United States of America
1 – PC – 7/15/14

# CONTENTS

CHAPTER ONE
RESPECT IS EARNED  4

CHAPTER TWO
CLIMBING THE RANKS  14

CHAPTER THREE
STAYING ON TOP  22

CHAPTER FOUR
STAYING STRONG  32

CHAPTER FIVE
AVOIDING INJURIES  40

CHAPTER SIX
THE BACKSTOP  48

Train Like a Pro  58

Hockey Equipment Diagram  59

Glossary  60

For More Information  61

Source Notes  62

Index  63

CHAPTER ONE

RESPECT IS

**H**ockey can be a brutal game. Players in the National Hockey League (NHL) are big, tough, and strong. One wrong play can result in a turnover. One wrong move can result in a check into the boards. It takes special talent to play in the NHL. To maintain a long career in the league requires a smart approach, a strong work ethic, and respect for the game.

It did not take long for Chicago Blackhawks center Jonathan Toews to show he belonged in the NHL. Toews had been known for his work ethic while growing up in Canada. His teammates and friends could see the focus he had to improve. And though he was a standout player, "Captain Serious" never acted like it.

Chicago Blackhawks center Jonathan Toews earned the respect of fellow players with his work ethic and humble approach to the game.

# EARNED

The Blackhawks noted his talent and his approach to the game. So the team selected Toews with the third pick in the 2006 NHL Entry Draft. He debuted for the Blackhawks in October 2007. The decision to pick him quickly paid off. Toews scored his first NHL goal on his first shot. Overjoyed, he immediately raised his hockey stick in celebration. His new teammates mobbed him.

The Blackhawks had known Toews was a special player when they drafted him. Fans quickly caught on. Toews excelled on the ice. He had 24 goals and 30 assists in 64 games that season. Toews also proved to be a natural leader. That showed when his Blackhawks teammates voted him captain for the 2008–2009 season. The captain is usually a veteran with a lot of experience. Toews was just 20 years old. No Blackhawks captain had ever been younger. But Toews proved he was up to the task.

Toews made the All-Star Game for the first time in 2009. Then he did the impossible. The Blackhawks had been miserable for most of the previous decade. They had made the playoffs just once since 1997. Fans were starting to stay away from

## Captains Are in Charge

Being named team captain is a big deal in hockey. That player wears a *C* on his jersey. He is the only player allowed to speak to the referees about rules. And the captain is a team leader. He is often the team's most visible player to the public as well. Teams also have two alternate captains. They wear an *A* on their jerseys. The alternates perform the captain's duty when the captain is not on the ice.

6

Blackhawks home games. Behind Toews, Chicago reached the playoffs again in 2009. Then the Blackhawks won the Stanley Cup in 2010 and 2013. Chicago had become a big-time hockey town once again.

As the Chicago Blackhawks' team captain, Jonathan Toews was the first player to lift the Stanley Cup after the team's victory in 2013.

## A Blue-Collar Sport

Hockey is one of the most popular sports in North America. However, professional hockey players have long been known for their humility. The best players are often the hardest-working players. Showboating is frowned upon. And anything less than full effort is unacceptable.

Players learn this approach from a young age. Hockey is an intense sport. A typical shift on the ice is less than one minute. Players are expected to go full speed throughout each shift. Hockey is also a physical game. Players get checked and sometimes even fight on the ice. A player who is not going all out is more likely to get injured. And a player who showboats is more likely to be targeted by opposing players.

Hockey coaches emphasize hard work and teamwork as players climb the ranks. Most hockey players develop outside of the spotlight. They play in front of small crowds in high school or junior leagues. The top prospects have to sit on long bus rides and carry their equipment just like everybody else. Players learn to trust their teammates while also taking personal responsibility for their actions.

## Born in Canada

Today's NHL teams play in fancy arenas on ice maintained by machines. But the sport began outside on natural ice.

As such, the sport's development occurred mostly in the colder cities of North America. Modern hockey was invented in Canada in the 1800s. The Stanley Cup also originated in Canada. Many amateur hockey teams were playing there by the 1890s. So Lord Stanley of Preston, the governor-general of Canada, purchased what is now known as the Stanley Cup. The Cup was first awarded to the amateur

## Quotable

*"Everything [Jonathan Toews] does presents [him] as the ultimate player. . . . Jonathan impacts [the] locker room. . . . He is the consummate player."*
—Los Angeles Kings coach and former NHL player Darryl Sutter

8

champion of Canada in 1893. The competition for the Stanley Cup has changed over the years. It eventually expanded to include professional teams and teams from

The Toronto Maple Leafs, *in white*, battle against the New York Rangers during the 1940 Stanley Cup Finals.

Maurice "the Rocket" Richard led the Montreal Canadiens to eight Stanley Cup titles between 1944 and 1960, including five in a row to end his career.

the United States. And since 1927, the Cup has been awarded to the NHL champion.

Other professional leagues existed before the NHL began in 1917. However, the NHL emerged as the dominant league. Yet even the NHL struggled to find stability in its early years. Various teams from northern US states and Canada came and went throughout the first 25 years. It was not until the 1942–1943 season that the league finally stabilized.

The league had six teams that year. And for the next 25 seasons, the Boston Bruins, the Blackhawks, the Detroit Red Wings, the Montreal Canadiens, the New York Rangers, and the Toronto Maple Leafs were the only teams in the league. Those teams became known as the Original Six. They set the foundation on which the NHL has grown.

## Dynasties

The NHL has been known for its amazing dynasties. In sports, dynasties are teams that win many championships in a short period of time. The Montreal Canadiens are the NHL's ultimate dynasty. They have won the Stanley Cup a record 24 times through 2013. They won five titles in the 1950s, five more in the 1960s, and then six in the 1970s. Montreal won all five titles from 1956 to 1960. The New York Islanders won four titles in a row from 1980 to 1983. Then the Edmonton Oilers won five in seven years from 1984 to 1990. The only other NHL team to win three in a row was the Toronto Maple Leafs, who did it during the 1940s and again during the 1960s.

The league doubled in size to 12 teams in 1967–1968. More teams joined the league in the decades that followed. The NHL has been known for its dynasties. Strong teams such as the Canadiens in the 1950s and the Edmonton Oilers in the 1980s helped grow the NHL's popularity.

The NHL is now bigger than ever with 30 teams. Teams are spread across the United States and Canada. Fans fill up fancy arenas and watch the games on television. Meanwhile, the league has grown outside of North America. Players from many countries in Europe compete for roster spots. More and more North Americans are playing hockey as well. As history has shown, however, making it in the NHL is about much more than one's ability on the ice.

# IN THE SPOTLIGHT

Nobody doubted Patrick Kane's ability. The Chicago Blackhawks picked the right wing first overall in the 2007 NHL Entry Draft. Kane then went on to help the Blackhawks win the Stanley Cup in 2010. He even scored the series-clinching goal. It was Chicago's first Stanley Cup victory since 1961. Some people questioned if Kane was performing to the best of his ability, though. He began his NHL career at the age of 18. His immaturity sometimes showed in his decisions on and off the ice.

In 2012–2013, the NHL players and owners disagreed about player salaries and other issues. Nearly half of the season was lost as they tried to make a deal. Kane decided to spend his time away from the NHL by playing with a team in Switzerland. He lived with his mom. It was a modest life with few distractions. But the experience helped Kane grow up. When the NHL season finally began, Kane had his best season yet. It ended with another Stanley Cup title.

# CHAPTER TWO

# CLIMBING THE

Getting to the NHL is a journey. Only a select few players are good enough to play in the NHL as teenagers. Most players need years to work their way up through the ranks. There are many paths a player can take to the NHL. Most player development takes place out of the spotlight, though. And dedication is essential for those who hope to reach the NHL.

The players who reach the NHL are highly skilled. They also must be versatile. Any weakness can easily be exposed once a player reaches the top level. Building one's skills usually starts at the youth level. And one of the first skills any player learns is skating. Skating is the foundation of hockey. A player who can skate well is more effective in all aspects of the game. So players who reach the NHL are expected to be in complete control on their skates. They must be well balanced and be able to turn and stop on a dime. Speed is also important. These skating skills come into play any time a player is on the ice. As such, even the best hockey players never stop working to improve their skating.

Center Steven Stamkos, opposite page, became a prolific scorer after the Tampa Bay Lightning selected him first overall in the 2008 NHL Entry Draft.

# RANKS

15

Players learn more hockey skills as they rise through the youth ranks. These skills include puck handling, passing, shooting, and checking. Eventually players begin to work on game strategy. Coaches develop tactics to help each line perform at its best. Many hockey players already possess strong fundamentals and a good understanding of the game by their teenage years.

## Different Directions

The level of play generally ramps up around the time kids begin high school. This is also where young players' paths usually begin to differ. Some states have great high school hockey leagues. For example, many of the best teenage players in Minnesota play on high school teams. But high school hockey is less developed elsewhere. So many top players aged 16 to 20 try out for junior teams. There are three tiers of junior leagues in the United States. The top tier is the United States Hockey League. However, the most competitive junior leagues are in Canada. These are called major junior leagues. These leagues attract great young players from around the world.

Junior hockey is a great commitment for young players. They often have to leave home to find a team. That means giving up a traditional high school experience. Family and friends are far away. Instead, the junior players live with team-sponsored families and attend local high schools.

Nail Yakupov watches his Sarnia Sting teammates play in the Ontario Hockey League, a major junior league in Canada, in 2012. The Edmonton Oilers selected Yakupov first overall in the NHL Entry Draft that summer.

The level of play in junior hockey is also much higher than in youth hockey. One reason is that junior leagues are selective. Only the best players make the teams. In addition, most junior players have physically matured. The teams emphasize strength and endurance training. This results in fast, physical game play.

The games and the lifestyle are not always glamorous in junior leagues. Players must adapt to new surroundings. They also must put more hours into the sport than ever before. For those who excel, though, junior hockey can be the gateway to the next level.

After junior hockey, players take different paths to the NHL. Players can enter the NHL Entry Draft at aged 18. However, drafted players do not necessarily join NHL teams right away. Some stay in the major junior leagues. Others go to college. NHL teams are not allowed to pay college players. However, the NHL team holds

## The NTDP

The best 17- and 18-year-old players in the United States have a unique opportunity. In 1996, USA Hockey created the National Team Development Program (NTDP). The NTDP is based in Ann Arbor, Michigan. Some of the top prospects from around the country move there. They live with host families, attend a local high school, and play a lot of hockey. The players compete against high-level junior competition. They also play against college teams and in international tournaments. Top coaches work with the players on hockey skills, strength, and tactics. This intense approach is meant to prepare the players for the rigors of college and pro hockey. So far it has worked. NHL teams have drafted more than 200 NTDP players.

onto a drafted player's rights while he is in college. And indeed, some players immediately turn professional.

Turning professional still does not always mean a ticket to the NHL, though. Most players have to start their

Former NTDP player Jacob Trouba puts on a Winnipeg Jets hat after the team selected him ninth overall in the 2012 NHL Entry Draft.

# IN THE SPOTLIGHT

In 2011, more than 30 percent of NHL players were born outside of North America. Some of these players came to North America to play junior or college hockey. Many were groomed at home, though. Washington Capitals left wing Alex Ovechkin grew up in Russia. As a teenager he played four seasons in Russia's professional league. He also starred for Russia's youth national teams. NHL scouts took notice of his blistering shot. The Capitals picked Ovechkin first overall in the 2004 NHL Entry Draft.

Ovechkin scored 371 goals over his first eight seasons in Washington. He is considered one of hockey's best goal scorers. Yet he has continued to work on rounding out his skill set. In 2012–2013, Ovechkin learned he had a habit of passing too hard. That made it difficult for teammates to handle the puck. So Ovechkin started practicing finesse passes. He was credited with 24 assists in 48 games during the season.

professional careers in the minor leagues. The American Hockey League (AHL) is the highest-ranked minor league. Each AHL team is affiliated with an NHL team. That means the NHL squad can oversee the development of its prospects. Until players reach certain experience milestones, the NHL team can move them between the NHL and the minors as it sees fit. More experienced players can be sent to the minor leagues as well, but other teams have an option to claim the player first.

Moving up the ladder in hockey is a challenge. According to the *Hockey News*, only 5 percent of college and major junior players ever play in the NHL. The difference often comes down to the little details—the fundamentals that players develop from their first days on skates.

CHAPTER THREE

# STAYING ON

**J**ust getting to the NHL is a challenge. Keeping a spot on an NHL roster can be just as hard. There are always new players looking to take that roster spot. And there is no shortage of distractions to pull a player off his game. A key to maintaining success is focus. Few have demonstrated that better than Sidney Crosby.

The Pittsburgh Penguins' center was a top prospect. Fans were predicting an amazing NHL career for Crosby when he was a teenager. But Crosby maintained his focus. He did not take it easy in the youth and junior ranks. He continued working to develop his skills. And he has maintained that work ethic since being the first pick in the 2005 Entry Draft.

Pittsburgh Penguins center Sidney Crosby brings the puck up the ice during a 2013 game.

TOP

23

Sidney Crosby scores a goal against the Toronto Maple Leafs in 2013.

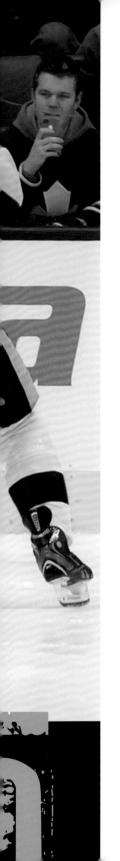

Crosby lifted the Stanley Cup for the first time at aged 21 in 2009. Yet he continued to try to improve. That year he won nearly 50 percent of his face-offs. Most players would be satisfied with such a high number. But Crosby was not. That summer he practiced face-off after face-off. The next season, in 2009–2010, he took 1,791 draws. It was the most of any player in the NHL. And Crosby improved his face-off percentage by more than 5 percent.

Crosby also worked to change his style. Some defenders had learned Crosby liked to pass more than shoot. That led to opposing defensemen backing off Crosby and guarding his teammates more closely. Crosby wanted to make himself more difficult to defend. So he spent many hours during the off-season taking shot after shot. The next season, Crosby tied for the league lead with 51 goals. It was an 18-goal improvement from the previous season.

The 2013–2014 season was Crosby's ninth in the NHL. He had already lived up to the high expectations from his teenage days. All of that success had made him into a big star. Reporters wanted to interview him. Companies wanted to work with

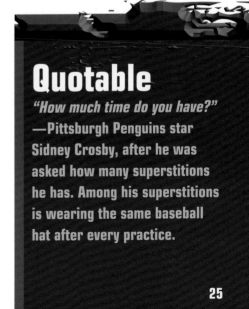

# Quotable

*"How much time do you have?"* —Pittsburgh Penguins star Sidney Crosby, after he was asked how many superstitions he has. Among his superstitions is wearing the same baseball hat after every practice.

him. Fans wanted to meet him. Meanwhile, his team and his fans expect him to deliver every night on the ice. All of that attention and pressure can take a player off his game. Not Crosby. He said he has learned to maintain focus on the single task at hand. Whether that task is a game, a practice, an off-season workout, or a public appearance, Crosby has a reputation for being prepared.

# Pregame Routines

It is an hour before opening face-off. Most players have their own activities to settle pregame nerves. Some like to jog or run for a few minutes. Then they stretch for another 10 minutes. Some goalies take time to bounce rubber balls off the wall. They practice catching the balls at different angles. The activity helps keep their reflexes sharp. Playing hallway soccer is another popular pregame activity, especially for European players. Players say it helps them improve their footwork and coordination. Generally, teammates form a circle and pass the ball back and forth. They attempt to keep the ball from hitting the hallway floor.

# A Day in the Life of an NHL Player

NHL players do a lot more than just play games. And game days are a lot more involved than simply playing three 20-minute periods.

Most NHL games are played at night. The players' workday starts several hours earlier at the morning skate. These early workouts are generally light practices. The morning skate helps the players loosen up and start mentally preparing for the game. Afterward, players generally return home or to the team hotel if they are on the road. After eating lunch, some players like to take afternoon naps. Increasingly, team officials spend extra time watching video and scouting the night's opponent.

Players must be back to the arena a few hours before opening face-off. Most have their own pregame routines. Players might stretch or do other activities to loosen up. Some players work with athletic trainers during this time. The trainers treat minor injuries so a player can still take the ice. In addition, coaches often address the team about the night's opponent.

After the game, the locker room is opened up to the media. Players and coaches are interviewed about the game and the season. The NHL requires teams to provide this media access. Players each have different postgame routines. Some just get dressed and leave the arena.

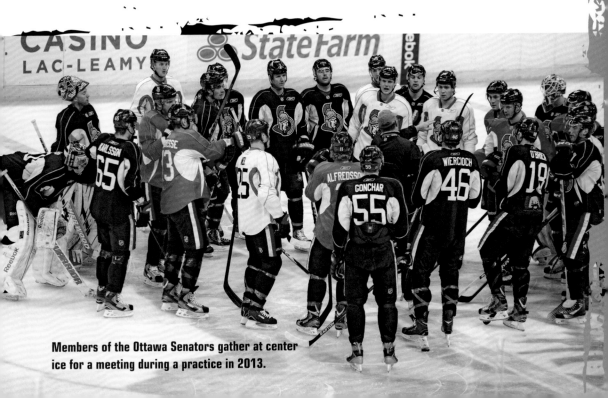

Members of the Ottawa Senators gather at center ice for a meeting during a practice in 2013.

Others ride stationary bikes to help cool down their muscles. Some players even do heavy weight lifting.

## Special Teams

Hockey has a unique system for dealing with penalties. A player who commits a penalty must go to the penalty box. His team must then play shorthanded. This is called a power play. The team missing a player is on a penalty kill. A minor penalty results in a two-minute penalty. The power play ends automatically if the full-strength team scores. Major penalties are five minutes. These continue even if the opposing team scores. Sometimes teams even get a five-on-three advantage if two opposing players commit penalties.

Power plays are great scoring opportunities. As such, teams often use their best offensive players in these situations. These players try to control the possession by passing in the offensive zone. The goal is to create an opening for the best possible shot.

Lifting right after a game gives the body maximum recovery time before the next game.

Most players finally leave the arena an hour or so after the game. But on the way out, they often double-check the next day's schedule. The daily grind continues.

Teams usually hold practices on days when there is no game. NHL practices generally begin at 10:00 in the morning. Most players arrive at the rink for practice at least an hour ahead of time. That gives them plenty of time to put on their equipment, stretch out, and prepare. Practices often start with warm-ups and work on fundamentals.

Montreal Canadiens defenseman P. K. Subban leaves the ice
after a Stanley Cup playoffs game in 2013.

The players might go through drills designed to improve their skating speed or shooting accuracy.

Coaches then divide the team into various groups, usually based on position or line. The groups run through situations and strategy for the next game. For example, a team might be in a power play slump. So during practice, that team might focus on power play situations. A team scrimmage often closes out practices.

Is the players' workday done after on-ice practice? Not by a long shot. When practice ends, weight training and endurance running begins. The most successful players are usually the ones who work just as hard off the ice as they do on it.

Maintaining this schedule for a week can be difficult. NHL players have to maintain it for approximately 28 weeks. Then, if they make the playoffs, the season can be extended another eight or nine weeks. In between games, teams have to travel hundreds of miles. During the 2013–2014 season, the San Jose Sharks were scheduled to travel 57,612 miles (92,718 kilometers). Even the New York Rangers, with the lightest schedule, traveled 29,839 miles (48,021 km) that year. All of that travel can take a toll on one's body. That makes maintaining a healthful lifestyle important for NHL players. It is important that they get enough rest and have a balanced diet. Not doing so can result in players becoming sluggish on the ice.

# IN THE SPOTLIGHT

The NHL has had its share of unique personalities. Many had their own distinct ways to help prepare for the drop of the puck. Hall of Famers Wayne Gretzky and Patrick Roy had some of the quirkiest pregame rituals of all time.

Gretzky is widely considered the greatest player to ever play the sport. Before each game, he always put on his equipment in the same order. It was left shin pad, left sock, right shin pad, right sock, pants, left skate, right skate, shoulder pads, left elbow pad, right elbow pad, then the jersey, with the right side tucked into his pants. Gretzky also sprinkled baby powder on his sticks.

Roy was a star goalie. He won a record 151 playoff games and four Stanley Cups. He never glided over any line on the ice during pregame skates. Instead, he hopped over them. Roy also spoke to the goalposts before the game. He said the posts "are my friends."

CHAPTER FOUR

# STAYING STRONG

**S**quats. One after another. For hours and hours and hours. That is what Chicago Blackhawks center Jonathan Toews does to build his leg muscles. He also does squats to increase speed, power, and endurance.

"I've done lots of squats these past three or four years because I'm focused on becoming a better skater, which means improving my quad strength," Toews said. "I'll do split squats, hack squats, all that type of stuff. I'll also do lots of cable pulls for my hips, my hip flexors and groin. If you're not strong enough, you're going to tear those because they get beat up over the season from playing so much hockey."

Jonathan Toews of the Chicago Blackhawks races after a loose puck during a 2013 game.

The upper body is important too. Several NHL teams encourage players to do circuit training in the weight room. Circuit training involves a variety of lifts in one session.

This helps the players get a full-body workout. Circuit training also helps with cardio since the athletes rush from one exercise to the next.

Toews concentrates on resistance-based interval training. It is intense. Toews uses light weights to work each muscle group. He does as many reps as he can for 30 seconds. Then he rests for 30 seconds. Toews's job is done when he completes work on all his muscle groups.

"The 30 seconds rest is almost as bad as the actual lifts because we know what's coming next," Toews joked.

Strength is important in hockey. Endurance is important too. NHL players average approximately 20 minutes of ice time per game. Yet each shift lasts only around 30 to 45 seconds. Players have to

## Eat Better, Play Better

Colorado Avalanche forward Matt Duchene wanted to get in better shape for the 2012–2013 season. So the 22-year-old maintained a strict sugar-free diet during the off-season. He went on to score 43 points in 47 games in 2012–2013. It was the best points-per-game average of his career. NHL players pay close attention to their diets. Many players avoid processed foods and sugars. Seeds, nuts, and whole-grain foods make more healthful snacks. Players also avoid sugary drinks such as soda. Drinking a lot of water is important, though. Popular pregame meals designed to provide energy include yogurt and whole-grain cereals. NHL players also eat nutrient-rich food such as steak, chicken, fish, pasta, fruits, and vegetables.

compete at full speed throughout their shifts. The players who remain fresh late in games have an advantage.

NHL players tailor their workouts to mimic a game. They practice the sudden bursts of exertion during a 45-second shift. One way they do this is by running

The Colorado Avalanche's Matt Duchene, *right*, works to keep possession of the puck during a 2013 game.

full-speed footraces. Each race lasts the time of a typical shift.

"I do a lot of sprints and foot races," Toews said. "I'll do drills on the tennis court with cones. We also do 400-meter (437-yard) sprints to get the breathing and aerobic system going. It's a lot of endurance stuff because the season is a marathon."

Technology has allowed for new training tactics. One such example is the off-ice skating treadmill. Players step onto the treadmill wearing skates. They then skate as fast as they can for several seconds. The treadmill allows players to skate at different degrees of difficulty. It helps improve the power and coordination of players' strides.

## Hockey Dedication

Any athlete must be committed in order to reach his or her full potential. In hockey, it is not uncommon for young players to have odd schedules. Ice time at rinks is expensive and sometimes limited. Many practices are staged early in the morning. The players

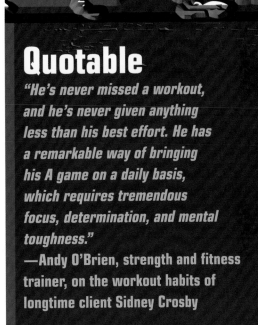

## Quotable

*"He's never missed a workout, and he's never given anything less than his best effort. He has a remarkable way of bringing his A game on a daily basis, which requires tremendous focus, determination, and mental toughness."*
—Andy O'Brien, strength and fitness trainer, on the workout habits of longtime client Sidney Crosby

37

arrive at the hockey rink as the sun begins to rise. Sometimes these practices take place on weekdays before school. This dedication is often necessary because there is no other option.

Players must remain focused once they reach the NHL. Hockey depends on players' ability to read plays quickly. Reactive drills help players respond to sudden changes. A popular drill is the box jump. The participant in this drill stands near a box. Then a coach or a teammate claps. At the sound, the player responds by jumping up on the box. Training partners clap at different times. It helps teach the player's brain to wait, anticipate, and react.

Skipping rope is helpful for hockey too. It is an old-school way to improve hand-eye and foot-eye coordination. Skipping rope helps improve foot speed. It also aids in endurance and agility. Many athletes like this exercise because it can be done almost anywhere.

# IN THE SPOTLIGHT

The Pittsburgh Penguins went into the 2013 Stanley Cup playoffs with high hopes. But the Boston Bruins swept the Penguins in the conference finals. Penguins center Sidney Crosby was crushed. He failed to score a goal or record an assist during the series. However, he did not dwell on the setback for long. He soon increased his training.

Crosby is known for his grueling off-season workouts. He has been working with training guru Andy O'Brien since he was 13. The two have developed an off-season routine that keeps Crosby fit. They concentrate constantly on improving Crosby's agility, speed, strength, and coordination.

Crosby often begins his daily training schedule by meeting up with friends and other NHL players. They run "killer" sand dunes before traveling to a gym. There, Crosby and company go through specific drills. The drills are designed to build strength and increase flexibility. Tumble push-ups and drop-unders are a few of the special core stability exercises O'Brien likes.

CHAPTER FIVE

AVOIDING INJURIES

**D**efenseman Bryan Berard was a top prospect. He was the first overall pick in the 1995 NHL Entry Draft. Then he claimed the 1997 Calder Trophy as the NHL's top rookie.

On March 11, 2000, Berard was a member of the Toronto Maple Leafs. His team was playing the Ottawa Senators. In an instant, his career changed. The stick of Senators forward Marian Hossa clipped Berard in the right eye. Berard was not wearing a visor. At the hospital, he learned he would lose a majority of his vision in that eye. Doctors even considered removing the eye. The injury should have ended Berard's career. But he immediately told family and friends that he would play again.

New York Islanders defenseman Bryan Berard, opposite page, skates during the 1996–1997 season.

41

Over the next year, Berard had seven eye operations. Finally, with the aid of a special contact lens, Berard was able to return to the NHL. Berard proved to be a serviceable defenseman upon his return. But he was never quite the same dynamic player. Still, he went on to play 329 games over six seasons after the injury. Berard was awarded the Bill Masterton Memorial Trophy in 2004. It honors a player's perseverance, sportsmanship, and dedication to hockey.

## Fighting

Many people believe the NHL does not do enough to discourage fighting. Opposing players occasionally drop their gloves and start punching each other. Fighting is a major penalty. That means both players go to the penalty box for five minutes. Some people argue that fighting helps police hockey games. For example, a player who targets an opponent's star player might become a target himself. But other people point out that fighting is dangerous. These people believe the punishment should be worse.

Similar injuries can happen at any time during a hockey game. Players are big and strong. Crashing into one another at high speeds is part of the game. And, all the players carry hockey sticks. Freak injuries are just part of the game.

That does not mean that all violent play is legal, though. The NHL bans plays such as tripping, hooking, slashing, high-sticking, and cross-checking. Players who violate

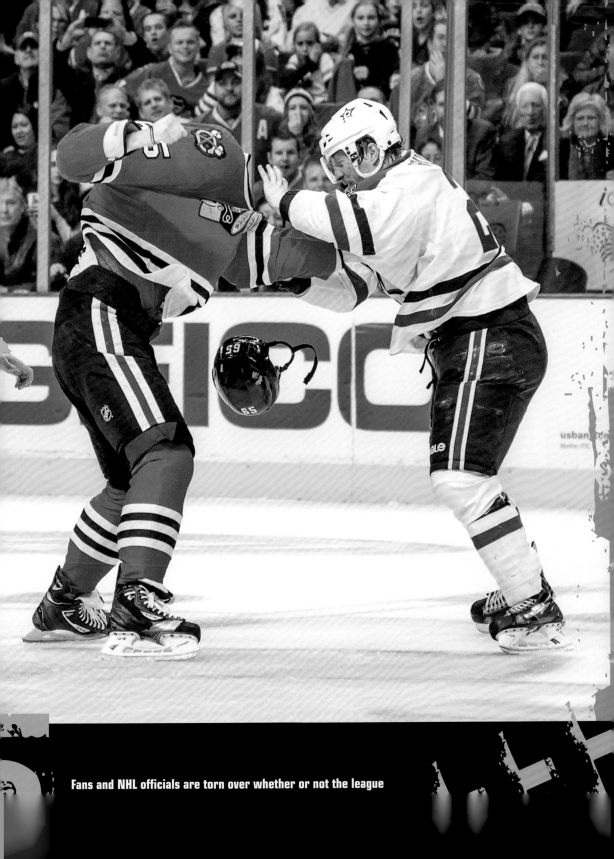

Fans and NHL officials are torn over whether or not the league

these rules are called for penalties. That means their team has to play shorthanded until their penalty expires. Sometimes players commit one of these penalties accidentally. They are punished nonetheless. The goal is to discourage players from playing in ways that could be dangerous to themselves and others.

## The Importance of Stretching

Some easy measures can help prevent injuries. One way to improve safety on the ice is by following the fundamentals. For example, players are reminded to skate with their heads up. Failure to do so puts the player at risk of a blindside hit. In addition, proper technique in giving and receiving a body check can limit the risk.

## Quotable

*"You just go out and play. I enjoy playing a lot of minutes; I feel like the more you play, the more you're into the game. I don't really have a routine. I just try to eat good and sleep when I can. It's all mental, I think."*
—Minnesota Wild defenseman Ryan Suter on how he prepares to play more than 27 minutes a game

Improved flexibility also helps avoid injuries. During each workout, muscles tear down. As the muscles recover, they tighten. Important muscle groups need to be stretched out daily. If not, a player's range of motion will be limited.

Players go through stretching routines before going on the ice. Three of the most important areas to stretch are the muscle groups of the groin, back, torso, and hamstrings.

Skating is not like running. Skating requires players to stretch their legs from side to side. That puts a lot of pressure on the groin area. There are different techniques for stretching out the groin while skating. For example, a player can drag one leg behind the body while bending as low to the ice as possible.

When shooting, the midsection goes through a strenuous twisting motion. If not properly stretched out, the back and torso can get injured. Players have different ways to stretch their midsections. One way is through trunk twists while holding a stick behind the back.

Montreal Canadiens defenseman P. K. Subban stretches before a 2013 game.

# IN THE SPOTLIGHT

Ryan Suter is not flashy. Yet his consistently strong play has earned him a reputation as one of the NHL's best defensemen. In 2012–2013, he averaged more than 27 minutes of ice time per game for the Minnesota Wild. That was the highest in the NHL. Sometimes Suter played much more. In one 2013 playoff game, Suter played more than 41 minutes. Those high numbers are rare in the NHL.

Suter excels in all hockey situations. He is skilled at bringing the puck out of the Wild's defensive zone. His big slap shot makes him a scoring threat. He also thrives on special teams. Suter plays on the Wild's power play and penalty kill units. And he is rarely called for a bad penalty.

"You're going to have good shifts, and you're going to have bad shifts," Suter said. "It's about the next shift. We can't get down."

Hamstrings are big muscles in the back of the leg. They allow players to generate power while skating. Stretching the hamstrings is simple. Players sit on the ground with one leg out and one leg in. Then they reach out and touch the toe of the far leg for several seconds.

Stretching before and after games helps prevent injuries. Stretching has other benefits too. It can help muscle recovery after a tough workout. Flexibility also improves speed and performance.

CHAPTER SIX

# THE BACKSTOP

**A** hockey goalie can make or break a team. The Los Angeles Kings found that out in 2012. The Kings entered that year's Stanley Cup playoffs as the eighth seed in the Western Conference. Few expected them to get out of the first round. Then goalie Jonathan Quick got hot.

Quick and the Kings lost just two games in the first three rounds of the playoffs. The Kings then dropped two games to the New Jersey Devils in the Stanley Cup Finals. But the Kings won four. Quick ended the playoffs with a 1.41 goals against average (GAA). His save percentage was an amazing .946. The performance earned Quick the Conn Smythe Trophy. That goes to the best player throughout the playoffs. More importantly, though, the Kings won their first Stanley Cup.

Los Angeles Kings goalie Jonathan Quick guards his goal during Game 4 of the 2012 Stanley Cup Finals.

49

The goalie is just one player on an NHL team. In fact, teams have 20 active players for each game. All but two of those players are forwards and defensemen. However, the starting goalie is the only one who usually plays the entire game. If the goalie is playing well, he leaves the game only for special circumstances. For example, a team trailing might pull the goalie late in the game for an extra attacker. The goalie is also a specialized position. These factors make a good goalie very important.

A goalie's job appears simple. He just has to stop shots from going into the goal. There is actually a lot more to the position, though. An NHL goalie must have excellent goaltending skills. But he also must be in great shape and make good decisions. In addition, goalies need to be mentally tough. Most goalies give up at least one goal per game. The test is how the goalie reacts afterward.

## The Positions

Each NHL team can have between 20 and 23 players on the active roster. However, only 20 players per team are allowed to dress for a given game. Two of those players must be goalies. Typically, teams will have 12 forwards and six defensemen. The forwards are split into four lines of three players. The defensemen are split into three pairs. Coaches try to organize the lines to include players with good chemistry. For example, the first line of forwards usually is a team's highest-scoring line. Teams also often have a checking line. These forwards are known more for their defense than offense.

# Getting Technical

The first thing most people notice is a goalie's style. A stand-up goalie stays on his skates to make most saves. A butterfly goalie often tries to stop shots from his knees. These goalies spread their leg pads to the side like

Jonathan Quick makes a save for the Los Angeles Kings during Game 4 of the 2012 Stanley Cup Finals.

butterfly wings. Most goalies today, however, have a hybrid style. That means they mix both stand-up and butterfly techniques.

Fitness is essential for goalies. Goalies do not have to skate up and down the rink like their teammates. But they are constantly on the move in other ways. Some of these movements are short bursts. Goalies glide back and forth across the crease to get into position. Goalies also must be able to quickly drop to their knees and then pop back up. All of this movement could be tiring in street clothes. NHL goalies must do it while wearing as much as 25 pounds (11 kilograms) of equipment. NHL goalies usually play all 60 minutes of a game, too.

New York Rangers goalie Henrik Lundqvist is one of the best netminders in the NHL. His workouts focus on three areas: cardio, strength training, and

## Goalie Equipment

Goalie equipment has gotten lighter and safer over the years. Today goalies wear a lot of padding, including a full helmet and large leg pads. Goalies also use a glove, a blocker, and a special stick to stop shots. However, there is a constant debate over how large goalie pads may be. Before the 2013–2014 season, the NHL decided goalie pads were too big. Goalies were forced to reduce the padding from the knee to the hip by 10 percent. That meant approximately 2 inches (5 centimeters) were shaved off each leg pad.

core. Cardio refers to one's heart rate. Lundqvist does short bursts of cardio workouts. These mimic the short bursts of movements during games. Stationary bikes are common for cardio workouts.

Goalies must be able to move quickly and powerfully. Strength training helps them do that. Lundqvist does workouts to build explosiveness in his legs. These workouts include squats and lunges. The core muscles are those in the torso. These muscles are important for balance and stability. They also help a goalie switch positions quickly during a game. Basic core muscle-building techniques include sit-ups and planks.

Flexibility is key too. Goalies go to great lengths to block the goal. They spread their legs wide and flop across the ice. Stretching exercises help build flexibility. Stretching also helps goalies avoid injuries.

## Smart Decisions

Not to be overlooked are a goalie's decision-making skills. Goalies are constantly making important decisions

## Quotable

*"Obviously it's a little smaller visually and when you put it on it feels a little smaller, but it's just an adjustment that goaltenders have to make."* —Chicago Blackhawks goalie Corey Crawford on the NHL's new restrictions for goalie equipment for the 2013–2014 season. To fit the new requirements, Crawford's leg pads were shortened from 38 inches (97 cm) to less than 36 inches (91 cm).

St. Louis Blues goalie Jaroslav Halak stretches out to block a shot against the Chicago Blackhawks' Dave Bolland

throughout a game. The offensive action in hockey is fast. Goalies have to be constantly aware of their surroundings. Correct positioning can be the difference between an easy save and an easy goal. The best NHL goalies learn to read the game over many years. They often study opposing teams to better understand the opponent's tendencies.

Goalies also have to decide the most effective way to stop a shot. A lot of goals come off rebounds. Giving up some rebounds is unavoidable. However, a well-prepared goalie can direct many of his rebounds. This limits easy second-chance opportunities.

In addition, goalies handle the puck throughout each game. Upon making a save, the goalie must make a decision. He can hold onto the puck and freeze it. Or he can keep the play going and pass the puck to a teammate. Goalies also routinely make plays on loose pucks around the goal.

The best NHL goalies have great natural ability. However, a lot of preparation and practice goes into maximizing those abilities.

# IN THE SPOTLIGHT

On November 1, 1959, Jacques Plante made history. The Montreal Canadiens' goalie had been hit in the face with a puck. That was hardly the first time that happened. Finally, he was fed up. So when Plante returned to the ice, he wore a full face mask. Other NHL goalies had reportedly worn face masks in the past. But Plante started a trend. Within a few years, most NHL goalies wore a mask.

Goalie masks have become far more sophisticated over the years. Plante's mask was made of fiberglass. The mask covered his entire face except for his eyes and part of his mouth. However, the sides and back of his head were still exposed. Today's goalie masks include a fitted helmet that covers the entire head and throat. On the front is a cage. The cage is safer and allows for more visibility than Plante's mask. Many NHL goalies hire professional artists to decorate their helmets.

# Train Like a Pro

## Crossover Lunge

Many hockey players, such as Pittsburgh Penguins center Sidney Crosby, do the crossover lunge to improve midsection flexibility. The exercise creates a fluid crossover motion needed for power skating. Runway space of about 30 feet (9 m) is required. To correctly execute the exercise, hockey players drive one knee up high and bring it across their bodies into a crossover position. Then lunge.

Players keep their hips, knee, and toes facing forward. The players then repeat the motion with their other knee and continue alternating for 15 lunges. Most do two sets.

# Hockey Equipment Diagram

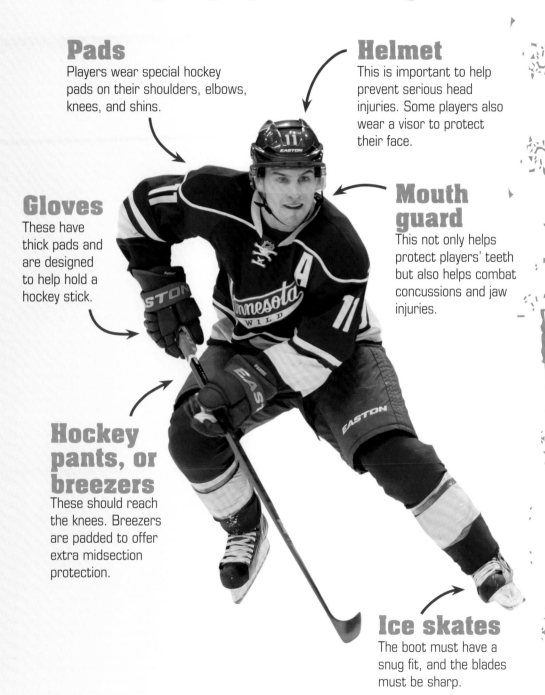

## Pads
Players wear special hockey pads on their shoulders, elbows, knees, and shins.

## Helmet
This is important to help prevent serious head injuries. Some players also wear a visor to protect their face.

## Gloves
These have thick pads and are designed to help hold a hockey stick.

## Mouth guard
This not only helps protect players' teeth but also helps combat concussions and jaw injuries.

## Hockey pants, or breezers
These should reach the knees. Breezers are padded to offer extra midsection protection.

## Ice skates
The boot must have a snug fit, and the blades must be sharp.

# Glossary

**affiliated:** when two independent things have a relationship

**amateur:** unpaid. Amateur athletes cannot earn compensation for their performance.

**assist:** a pass or passes that directly lead to a goal. A limit of two assists can be awarded per goal.

**body check:** the act of a player bumping or slamming into an opponent with a hip or shoulder

**crease:** the area in front of the goal. Opponents cannot obstruct the goalie in this space.

**dynasty:** a team that wins many championships over a short period of time

**endurance:** the ability to perform for an extended period

**face-off:** the act of starting play when a referee drops the puck between two opposing players

**junior:** a stage of hockey for players ages 16 to 20. Many junior leagues exist in the United States and Canada.

**off-season:** the time of year when a league is inactive

**penalty:** an illegal action in a game that results in time spent in the penalty box

**prospect:** a young player with potential to play in the NHL

**rookie:** a first-year player in the NHL

**superstition:** an irrational belief or practice

**veteran:** a player who has lots of experience

# For More Information

Hockey Hall of Fame
http://www.hhof.com
Learn all the facts and study the stats of the Hall of Famers, ice hockey's greatest players.

Kennedy, Mike, and Mark Stewart. *Score! The Action and Artistry of Hockey's Magnificent Moment*. Minneapolis: Millbrook Press, 2011.
This book tells readers all about scoring. It includes stories of iconic goals as well as goal-scoring technique.

Morrison, Jessica. *Wayne Gretzky: Greatness on Ice*. New York: Crabtree Publishing Company, 2011.
This biography tells the story of Wayne Gretzky. Many consider him to be the best NHL player ever.

National Hockey League
http://www.nhl.com
Visit this site for updated information on the National Hockey League.

USA Hockey
http://www.usahockey.com
This site has all the information on USA Hockey programs around the country.

# Source Notes

8   Tim Sassone, "Blackhawks MVP? It's Got to Be Toews," *Daily Herald* (Suburban Chicago), April 18, 2013, http://www.dailyherald.com/article/20130418/sports/703189550.

25  Hooks Orpik, "When It Comes to Superstitions, Sidney Crosby Leads the Way Here Too," *SB Nation: Pensburgh*, May 8, 2013, http://www.pensburgh.com/2013/5/8/4313966/when-it-comes-to-superstitions-sidney-crosby-leads-the-way-here-too.

31  Barry Meisel, "Dueling Goalies Roy, Vanbiesbrouck Are Keys In Wales Finals," *Philly.com*, May 6, 1986, http://articles.philly.com/1986-05-06/sports/26049966_1_john-vanbiesbrouck-patrick-roy-rangers.

33  Jon Finkel, "Windy City Warrior," *Muscle & Performance,* March 2010, http://www.muscleandperformancemag.com/departments/profile/2010/3/windy-city-warrior.

34  Ibid.

37  Ibid.

37  Jeff Angus, "An Interview with Fitness Coach Andy O'Brien," *Angus Certified*, October 26, 2012, http://www.anguscertified.com/an-interview-with-fitness-guru-andy-obrien/.

39  "Sidney Crosby Hosts the Best Pick Up Game. Ever," *Sidelines*, August 1, 2013, http://sidelines.sportsblog.com/post/132852/sidney_crosby_hosts_the_best.html.

44  Rachel Blount, "Suter Thrives Playing 'Crazy' Minutes for Wild," *Minneapolis StarTribune*, May 3, 2013, http://www.startribune.com/sports/wild/205902451.html.

46  Ibid.

54  Kevin Woodley, "NHL Goalies Weigh In after Trying New Smaller Pads," *InGoal Magazine*, August 24, 2013, http://ingoalmag.com/news/nhl-goalies-finally-get-to-try-out-new-smaller-pads/.

# Index

Berard, Bryan, 41–42

captains, 6
college hockey, 18–19, 20, 21
Crawford, Corey, 54
Crosby, Sidney, 23–26, 37, 39

Duchene, Matt, 34
dynasties, 11, 12

fighting, 42
fitness, 33–38, 50, 53–54

Gretzky, Wayne, 31

history, 8–12

injury prevention, 42–47, 54

junior hockey, 8, 16–18, 20, 21, 23

Kane, Patrick, 13

Lundqvist, Henrik, 53–54

minor leagues, 21

NHL Entry Draft, 6, 13, 18–19, 20, 23, 41
NTDP (National Team Development Program), 18
nutrition, 34

Original Six, 11
Ovechkin, Alex, 20

Plante, Jacques, 57
positions, 50

Quick, Jonathan, 49

Roy, Patrick, 31

special teams, 28, 30, 44, 46
Stanley Cup, 7, 8–11, 13, 25, 31, 39, 49
superstitions, 25, 31
Suter, Ryan, 44, 46
Sutter, Darryl, 8

Toews, Jonathan, 5–7, 8, 33–34, 37

workouts, 28, 30, 33–38, 39, 54

# About the Author

Jeff Hawkins is a writer who resides in Huntersville, North Carolina. Hawkins is a former award-winning sportswriter who covered the NHL's Chicago Blackhawks (2003–2006) and United Hockey League's Adirondack IceHawks (1999–2003). A Michigan native, Hawkins grew up a fan of the Detroit Red Wings.

# Photo Acknowledgments